Blend Hunt

Set 3

Written by Kassi Gilmour

Practise the sounds

m s t a p i f c r o d h e

n g k ck u l ll b j w wh y

The Blend Hunt books are designed to help children practise blending new sounds within each set. Once each word is successfully blended, children search for the item that matches the words they have read on each page.

Practise tricky words

I my the is a

he she me we

to do you was no go

Blend Hunt
Set 3

Written by Kassi Gilmour

run   hill

jet bell click

pink rocks
bag

pink lamp
clock

rod   pond   net

red jet
land

gift bag
flag

wet dog

pond   rocks

cod   frog   mug

Fin 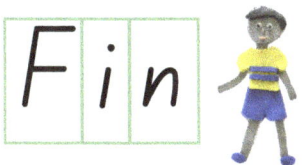 Sam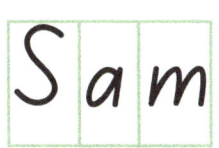

Pam's Dog

Written by Kassi Gilmour

Practise the sounds

m s t a p i f c r o d h e

n g k ck u l ll b j w wh y

Practise blending sounds

P	am	

d	o	g

w	a	g	s

p	e	t

w	i	n	s

h	i	ll

p	o	n	d

s	o	f	t

t	e	ll	s

Practise tricky words

I my the is a

he she me we

to do you was no go

Pam's Dog

Set 3

Written by Kassi Gilmour

Pam has a pet dog.

The dog is big.

Pam and the dog run up a hill.

The dog wins.

He jumps in a pond.

He gets wet.

Pam and the wet dog jog back.

When Pam gets back,
she gets the dog a snack.

She rubs him.

He is glad and wags!

Pam tells the dog to go to bed.

He hops into his soft bed.

Questions:

1. What does Pam do with her dog?
2. How does the dog get wet?
3. How does Pam feel about her dog?
4. What do you do for your pets?

Pam's Gift

Written by Kassi Gilmour

Practise the sounds

m s t a p i f c r o d h e

n g k ck u l ll b j w wh y

Practise blending sounds

| P | a | m | | g | i | f | t | | r | i | p | s |

| b | a | g | | h | e | l | p | | d | e | s | k |

| l | a | m | p | | p | i | n | k | | g | l | a | d |

Practise tricky words

I my the is a

he she me we

to do you was no go

Pam's Gift

Set 3

Written by Kassi Gilmour

I am Kass.

On my desk is a gift.

We go to Pam's.

I hand the gift to Pam.

She is glad to get the gift.

Pam rips the pack off.

It is a pink lamp.

I hug Pam.

She sets the lamp up on the desk.

Questions:

1. Where does Kass go?
2. Why is she going to Pam's house?
3. How does Pam feel?
4. What gifts have you given your friends?

The Jet

Written by Kassi Gilmour

Practise the sounds

m s t a p i f c r o d h e

n g k ck u l ll b j w wh y

Practise blending sounds

| F | in |

| j | e | t |

| o | ff |

| r | e | d |

| b | e | ll |

| s | p | e | d |

| l | o | ck |

| w | e | n | t |

| c | l | i | ck |

Practise tricky words

I my the is a

he she me we

to do you was no go

The Jet

Set 3

Written by Kassi Gilmour

Sam and Fin spot a jet.

The jet is big and red.

Sam gets in the jet.

He locks the jet.

Fin is not in the jet yet.

He frets and clicks the jet bell.

Sam lets Fin in.

The jet sped off on a fun trip.

Questions:

1. Where are Sam and Fin?
2. What does Sam do?
3. Why does Fin fret (worry)?
4. Have you ever been in a jet?

Pink Rocks

Written by Kassi Gilmour

Practise the sounds

m s t a p i f c r o d h e

n g k ck u l ll b j w wh y

Practise blending sounds

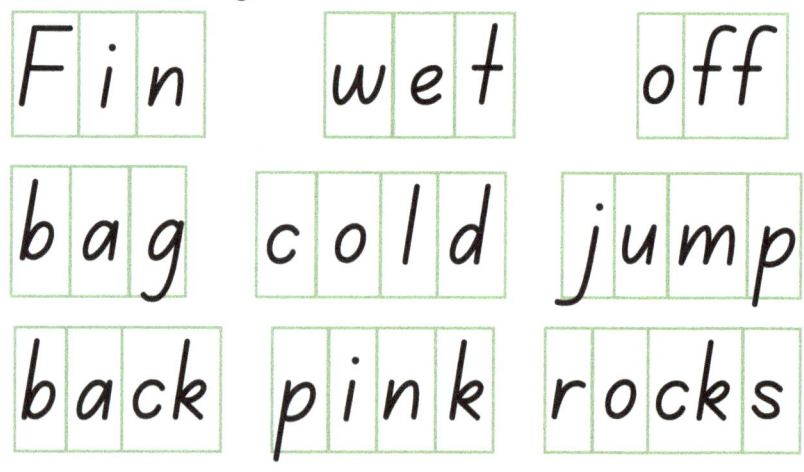

Practise tricky words

I my the is a

he she me we

to do you was no go

Pink Rocks

Set 3

Written by Kassi Gilmour

Sam and Fin hop off the jet.

It is cold and wet.

Sam picks up pink rocks, and Fin packs the bag.

When the rocks fill the bag, Fin drops the bag.

He has a rest.

Sam and Fin jump back on the jet.

The red jet sets off.

The jet lands.

No! The pink rocks did not go in the jet.

Questions:
1. Where did Sam and Fin go?
2. What did they do there?
3. Why does Fin put the bag down?
4. How do Sam and Fin feel when they return?

Cod

Written by Kassi Gilmour

Practise the sounds

m s t a p i f c r o d h e
n g k ck u l ll b j w wh y

Practise blending sounds

can not cannot
rod hops back
pond slip swims

Practise tricky words

I my the is a
he she me we
to do you was no go

Cod

Set 3

Written by Kassi Gilmour

Sam, Fin and Pam go to the pond.

A cod is in the pond.

Fin has a rod.

The cod jumps back.

Fin cannot get the cod.

Pam has a go.

The cod nips, but swims off.

Sam hops into the pond. He has a net.

He gets the cod in the net.

Sam slips and the cod jumps back into the pond.

We cannot get the cod.

Questions:

1. Where does Sam, Fin and Pam go?
2. What did they take with them?
3. Did they catch the cod fish?
4. Have you ever been fishing?

www.ingramcontent.com/pod-product-compliance
Lightning Source LLC
Chambersburg PA
CBHW042131100526
44587CB00026B/4261